TO MOVE OR NOT TO MOVE TO LA?

TO MOVE OR NOT TO MOVE TO LA?

ONE ACTOR'S JOURNEY TO FIND THE ANSWER

GERI PAYAWAL

Copyright © 2005 by Geri Payawal.
ISBN: 1-4134-5863-7

All rights reserved. No part of this book may be reproduced or transmitted in any form or by any means, electronic or mechanical, including photocopying, recording, or by any information storage and retrieval system, without permission in writing from the author.

This book was printed in the United States of America.

DEDICATION

B ~ For your never-ending support and belief . . . I love you.
You make my dreams possible.

To all my fellow actors who have the courage and determination
to live your dreams, no matter where you are, you inspire me everyday.

Introduction

The most important goal is not only to make it, but to enjoy the journey.

I set out on what most consider to be the impossible: Be a Movie Star! Okay, I KNOW . . . how many times have you heard that before, right? But how many times have you dreamed of this yourself? Is it really so impossible??? Okay yes, maybe for some, but *obviously* there is another side that DOES make it. So let me find a way to get myself on the side that does! We see it happen everyday . . . new up and coming faces who rise from, "Hey I just did an under five!" to "I'd like to thank the Academy . . ." I ask who, what, when, where, why not me!

Okay, putting the whole "movie star" thing aside, what really matters most to me is to be a consistently employed *paid* actress doing good work and work that I love, not in the background, but on the front line. It would be so great to book that two year, four year, *any* year contract role and not have to worry about a "money" job. I have been acting in New York for several years and have steadily been receiving work in stage, film and television (mostly for little or no pay) and often doing lots (LOTS) of background work for "extra" money (can't bite the hand that feeds ya). My resume does not claim to boast what is considered high caliber roles in the industry (yet), but it is respectable and continues to keep me working. I certainly do have my dry spells, but I manage to keep afloat. Lately however, I have been itching for something . . .

As much as I LOVE New York and consider it to be home in my heart, I needed, I wanted to open the doors to other opportunities; opportunities that may lead to those high caliber parts. Yes, there certainly are opportunities in New York, but by sheer numbers alone, if I want a career in film and television, I must look West. I'm not really sure how I got here. All I know is that the wheels have been set in motion. I am finally going to Hollywood!

This is a diary of my journey.

I decided to write this diary so that I can document my trip and also because I find writing to be very therapeutic. However the more I thought of it, the more I realized that this diary may help other actors who are thinking about making the move to LA. When I was first researching going out there, I found many books on LA agents and casting directors and actors' guides to LA, the city. What I didn't find was a book that described a New York actor's personal experience with the decision to head to LA. There well may be such a book, but the key word here is "personal." So even if there is another such book, this is *my* experience and for that reason, this book, as am I, is unique.

This diary is not intended and was not written to tell you what to do or how to do it. It is simply meant to tell my story. If along the way it helps or provides some guidance, or even some amusement, then I am happy to have been of service.

So, let's start from the beginning.

Too many times have I heard the warnings: *Don't go to LA unless you have an agent out there, don't go because the competition is fierce, don't go because everyone out there is an actor.* Well I finally got tired of all the "don'ts" and I was ready to DO. I realized that not going to LA because someone tells me not to go is the stupidest reason of all. So what if I have no LA agent (yet). I didn't have one when I first started acting in New York, yet I hustled and eventually freelanced with several agents here in the Big Apple. So I will work and hustle in LA too! Competition is fierce everywhere and yes, there are tons of actors in LA, but think of this—the reason why most actors flock there is because there is more work. It's just basic numbers—right now, more film and television shows are shot in LA. So rather than thinking glass half empty, think glass half full!! Half of succeeding in this business, heck, any business, is a positive attitude! The point is I am not going to listen to other people's perception of what it's "like" out there, I am going to find out for myself.

The past few weeks have seemed like a blur, working on mailings, ordering pictures, researching LA agents and casting directors, researching where to live in LA, and oh yeah, quitting my job. I can't forget that. Most normal people would think I'm crazy, but let's face it, choosing to be an actor is not exactly choosing a "normal" life. Most, scratch that, ALL actors know what I'm saying! Ours is a business of risks, nothing is ever certain or shall I say it, "stable." But we keep at it. Why??? For me it's a chance to fulfill a dream . . .

Before we begin this journey, let me back track a bit with a summary of events that brought me here as well as the planning and preparation involved.

MOTIVATING FACTORS:

- **Class at Actors Connection (NYC) with Brette Goldstein, Independent Casting Director (September-October 2003)**

Above all else, this class was the fuel that lit the flame for this trip. I signed up for this class as it had been a while since I'd been in an acting class. Class, especially if you're not working in a play or a film is so important because it allows you to keep learning and growing as an actor. I had been terribly guilty of letting myself get lazy in this respect so I was very eager to get back in there and work. It is very easy to let classes take a backseat, but here I stress that I made a big mistake taking a break from it for so long. I know for many of us, funds are an issue, and for me, that more so than anything else was the reason I stopped. I know now that it is an investment that cannot be overlooked, not only because it is a means by which we continue to improve our craft, but also because it provides an environment where you can be among peers who suffer the same struggles and celebrate the same joys that this business brings. When I was in this class I remembered how great it was to see other people's work and how fulfilling it is to get back up there and perform. The class was titled "Audition Breakthrough" but it incorporated monologues, cold readings and the business of acting. Brette was an amazing teacher not only because she gave honest, constructive feedback in a nurturing environment, but what made her memorable was that she truly took the time or simply, that she gave a shit.

There was this one class. It was a cool, rainy Sunday afternoon, and I remember this because it was my birthday, October 12. Brette gave me a great gift of advice that day.

It was a makeup class and there were just a handful of us in attendance. As such, there was extra time to address individual questions about acting and the business. So I asked the question that so many actors struggle with: LA vs. NY? Well as a New York based actress, I have often wondered whether the opportunities are greater out in the West Coast for someone pursuing a career in film and television. As the numbers alone show, the majority of these projects are filmed in LA. However on the flip side, there is also the fact that there are a huge number of actors who flock to LA for that reason which makes the competition even fiercer. The answer to my question was that, yes, if an actor wants a career in film and TV, they at least have to see what LA is all about. My teacher Brette is the one who planted this seed in my head: *Don't buy a ticket yet, but instead, send a mailing to LA and see if you get any bites.* This was all I needed to hear.

At that moment, something clicked for me and I thought, what do I have to lose?

- **New Year**

When I made the decision to follow my teacher's advice, I actually decided to take it a step further. For some reason, as we were approaching the 2004 New Year, I was ready to make some changes and fulfill some long, thought out goals. I decided that I was going to go to LA whether or not I got any "bites." I was too impatient and excited that rather than waiting to be invited out there, I got the ball rolling and bought my tickets. This was obviously a personal decision and I do not recommend for everyone to just get up and go. Each person has to consider their own situation and of course assess their finances and make that decision on their own. Even though I made a quick decision to buy my tickets, there was still a heck of a lot of planning that I needed to take care of before I made the trip and I only had about 2 months to do it! For me there was no question—I was going to LA. It's important to note, however, that this was a "feeler" trip for me. Although my decision may seem impetuous and spontaneous, I am still a "safety" girl at heart and so I did not pack up all my belongings and decide to relocate (at least not yet anyway). Instead I was going on I guess what you'd call a "research" expedition to see if LA is a place I could *live*. I gave myself about one month from the date of arrival to find out.

So, as it often happens with the approach of a New Year, many are encouraged to start new adventures. And so it was the case for me.

- **Quit Job**

Before I go into this, I want to make it very clear that I am not advocating for people to quit their jobs. This was something that I was ready to do. When I first decided that I wanted to pursue acting (this was back in 1997), I jumped into it full-steam ahead. I realized that there were too many people pursuing this 110% that I couldn't do it half-assed. So I quit my very "stable" job, and without any experience, went out in search of work in a restaurant—almost every actor's choice of the "money job" while pursuing acting.

But back to the present. I was very lucky to have later found a front-desk / administrative position with a firm that allowed me to go on auditions and shoots. The arrangement was that if I were to leave for an audition, I would just make up the time by coming in earlier the next day or leaving later the same day, and/or if I were to be out for a shoot, I would not get paid for that day. I considered this to be more than a fair trade as I was looking for a change from the restaurant business which I had been doing for nearly four years. This job was a gold mine as I was able to have a steady job while still having the flexibility to do my thing. This set-up is RARE. Why did I quit? Well, I had been with the company for almost three years and I was beginning to put my job responsibilities ahead of my acting. I was getting more involved with the company that sometimes when I would receive an audition call, I would second guess whether or not I should go because they needed me at the office. This was not the company's fault. I did this to myself. They never denied me the time to leave if I had to go to an audition, plus they knew from the get go that that is what I do and agreed to that when they first hired me. I know I shouldn't have felt guilty for having to leave for auditions and shoots, but as my responsibilities increased, I found more and more that my commitment to the company was getting in the way of my true goals. It was apparent that I was going to have to reevaluate my priorities.

It turned out that the timing was just right. Deciding to go to LA was the jumpstart I needed to focus my priorities back to my acting, and in turn provided me with a gracious way to hand in my notice.

- **Pilot Season**

Another incentive to head West was that Pilot Season (January-April) was approaching. Again, the timing worked out that I would arrive in LA just as Pilot Season kicked off. When I spoke to my friend Donna who has been out in LA for a couple of years (she made the move to LA from NY), she did mention that Pilot Season was a tough time to land an agent. The reason for this is because most agents already have their core talent that they need to focus on for potential pilots. As such, they do not have time to see or take on any new clients.

While planning this trip, the various books I read often suggested that the best time to go to LA was around May or Episodic Season. During that time, agents are winding down from Pilot Season and are weeding out those clients who did not "book" so perhaps they may be more inclined to look at fresh faces. I definitely took all of these thoughts into consideration, but when I made the decision to go to LA, I always remained in the mind frame of "hopeful, but realistic." I figured that whether or not I'm lucky enough to even be considered for representation, that this was still a good time to be in LA as there was a lot of activity and buzz happening. Also, this was more than a "landing an agent" trip for me, it was also an opportunity to see if I could be happy living in LA. So for those whose main goal is to land an agent, maybe the best time to head out to LA is in May when agents are more open to considering new talent. Granted, that is a definite goal for me too, but I just couldn't wait. At this stage, there was no turning back. I got my tickets. I was going.

- **New SAG Member**

A huge factor that was also a motivating force to head to LA was that I recently (finally!) joined the illustrious Screen Actors Guild (SAG). I was Union! I tell ya that was very exciting for me because it took me six years to get my SAG card. Here is another area where this business can be so random and unpredictable. Putting in the same hard work, some actors are fortunate enough to get their card within the first year, even the first month of pursuing this career, whereas some actors like me sometimes wait years for the honor.

So let's see, the Union question. I am not going to tackle this in depth because there are so many different viewpoints on the topic. What I can answer from my experience is that, yes, the level of respect you get as an actor definitely steps up quite a notch—that is my opinion. Being in SAG sends the message that you are a professional working actor. That of course is NOT to say that non-union actors don't work and are not professional. I can guarantee that most non-union actors definitely are. I was once non-union and I worked damn hard! All I can say is that being in the Union sets you apart. You ask any non-union actor if they would join SAG if offered, I would bet (without taking into consideration financial ability) that an overwhelming majority would jump on board. Why? Because it is a sort of, right of passage in the industry. All I know is that I worked hard to get into SAG and for anyone who wants a career in this business, getting into the Union is a must. Some may argue that it isn't, but this is a business of a million different opinions. Everyone is entitled to what they believe and where their goals lie. There are definitely some who are quite snobby about this status (I've met more than my fair share), but those people need to get a grip and remember that they were all once non-union too. I am now a proud Union member, but I will never forget where I came from. How can you forget working sometimes over 14 hours in one day as an extra for a mere base pay of $75 before taxes!

I remember when I was non-union, I was always in some kind of awe of SAG members, hungry to find out how they did it. At shoots discussions almost always found their way to this topic where you'd often hear, "So how did you get your SAG card?" or "How long did it take?" or "What steps can I take to get my card?" It was all this mystery, this illusive invitation to an elite group. Then there are the separate catering tables. I never understood that. But as a new SAG member, maybe now I will. It's all pretty crazy. I can't answer if there is more work out in LA if you're Union because I too have yet to find out. I think perhaps that there might be a disadvantage if you're non-union. On the flip side, I heard that it is easier to get your card in LA because there is more work. All I can say for sure is that being in the Union guarantees better pay and better working conditions. For me, getting my SAG card was another motivating factor in heading out to LA. It certainly couldn't hurt.

How did I get my SAG card? Well believe it or not, it was thanks to Big Bird and a really inspiring book titled, *"The Theatrical Juggernaut (The Psyche of a Star)"* by Monroe Mann. In this book he says if you really want something bad enough, you can and will find a way to get it. It is a very motivating book. He says that you must be "unstoppable" when it comes to making your dreams come true because that is *The Psyche of a Star*.

I booked a part as a Chorus Singer on Sesame Street's 35th Anniversary home video, *"What's the Name of that Song?"* I shot a scene opposite Big Bird—the most fun ever! The bit is that this police officer and I are humming a song and Big Bird asks "What's the name of that song?" and we say, "What's the Name of That Song?" (which is what the title of the song is) and he's like but I already asked you that! So the gag continues. Well, since I thought that this had to constitute as a speaking part, I called SAG and inquired if that made me eligible. They replied no because it was not considered a principal part. Basically one of the ways you can become eligible to join SAG is if you book an under five or principal part on an AFTRA (American Federation of Television and Radio Artists) job while being an AFTRA member for at least one year. Well thinking there was nothing else to be done, I disappointedly accepted that response without even going over my contract and let the issue drop. A few weeks went by and one day I was doing background work on a soap and as it often happens, actors talk and discuss the business. I happened to overhear another actor mention how much she got paid to work as an under five. After I heard the response, it dawned on me that I made a much higher rate working on Sesame Street! So my wheels started churning frantically . . . if I made more as a chorus singer than an under five role, why am I not eligible to join SAG? This did not make sense to me. Clearly if I was paid a higher rate then the part had to have been a level above an under five and further, if an under five made someone eligible to join SAG, then whatever contract I had on Sesame Street should most definitely qualify me to join the Union. At about the same time these thoughts were dancing in my head, I was reading *The Theatrical Juggernaut* and I remembered that very powerful message from the book that if you want something bad enough, you will find a way to get it.

With renewed determination I called the SAG office again the following day armed with a copy of my contract at hand and the mindset that I will not take no for an answer. I was a woman on a mission! I spoke with the membership office with an unwavering agenda and clearly explained what I did on Sesame Street and detailed the information on my contract. He said, "Yes, you are absolutely eligible." To my amazement the only question he asked me was when I wanted to set up an appointment to JOIN! Yep, he just said to bring the contract, my AFTRA card, a headshot and of course, a check and that he would see me in membership. WHOOPIE!!! I was floored! To think that I let it go the first time and just accepted that the answer was no without even questioning it.

This was such a great learning experience in fighting for what you want and not taking no for an answer. This was a great lesson in being "unstoppable."

Things to Plan and Prepare

Now that you have some of the reasons I was motivated to go to LA, here are some of the elements that I considered before I headed for my trip. Some may choose to prepare all or some of these details before making the trip, but it all depends on the length of your stay, the *funds* you have to spend (important!), and the goals you have for the trip. The key is to be as prepared as you can be. These steps all proved very helpful for me.

- **Mailings**

My flight to LA was on January 9. Below is a breakdown of the mailings I sent out prior to my trip. I admit I went a little crazy, but I knew nothing of LA and I certainly didn't know which agents and casting directors were the key movers and shakers so I pretty much sent it to almost everyone. Here I used the Ross Reports as my guide. For those of you who are not familiar with the Ross Reports, it is essentially a trade directory that lists all of the agents and casting directors for each state along with all the shows and films currently in production. That is just some of the information you'll find in the Ross Reports. You can find it in most bookstores and select newsstands.

Initial Mailings

November 25, 2003	Agents	101 Headshots
November 25, 2003	Casting Directors (CD's)	25 Headshots
November 26, 2003	Primetime Casting Directors	44 Headshots
December 1, 2003	Additional Casting Directors	36 Postcards
December 5, 2003	Additional Agents	20 Headshots
December 8, 2003	Additional Casting Directors	42 Postcards
December 10, 2003	Additional Casting Directors	51 Headshots
December 11, 2003	Soap Opera Casting Directors	5 Headshots
December 12, 2003	Additional Primetime CD's	18 Postcards
December 12, 2003	Additional Agents	15 Postcards

Follow Ups:

December 16, 2003	Agents	101 Postcards
January 3, 2004	Agents, CD's and Primetime CD's	345 Postcards

Like I said, I went a little nuts with my mailing. My main thinking was that I wanted to cover everyone I possibly could. As far as who received headshots versus who received postcards, it was all very random. Postcards were sent mainly to save a bit of money as they are cheaper to reproduce and mail. So when you look at the breakdown and ask why some casting directors and agents were sent postcards, it was merely an effort to lower costs and certainly not because they were lower priority. As I said earlier, being a newbie to LA there was no way for me to know who the key players were. The only exception to that was when it came to the Primetime Casting Directors and the Soap Opera Casting Directors. I made it a point to send headshots to those offices rather than just postcards mostly because they were casting directors of already established shows. If you see the LA section of the Ross Reports, it literally covers a gazillion pages of agents and casting directors. It's insane how many more of these agencies and offices there are out in LA as opposed to NY. I would have gone nuts researching each and every one. The big names were easy enough to separate: ICM, Gersh, William Morris, etc, but hey, who is kidding who here— an unknown actress like me would be best suited for a smaller house agency to help me build substantial credits before these bigger agencies would even bat a Hollywood eyelash at me. But nevertheless, as this business is very unpredictable, I sent to both the big and small. I targeted everyone.

In regard to cost, I spent a pretty penny on reproductions and postage as well as supplies. Obviously it's important to consider how much time and money you have to spend on these mailings and still have enough money left over to survive when you're out there. I'm not encouraging everyone to go as massive on their mailings as I did. I may have gone overboard, but for me, since I absolutely had no contacts out there, it was what I considered the key to getting my face seen. Since I was fortunate enough to have had a stable job earning a steady income before I decided to head out there, I did have some savings that I was able to rely on to do such a massive mailing. It is really important to take into consideration ALL costs *before* the trip (headshot reproductions, mailings, airline tickets, etc.) and especially *during* your stay (rent, car, parking, food, etc.)—

reviewing all of these factors with your finances in mind will help determine how much you are able to spend on a mailing.

As far as timing goes, I sent out an initial mailing about one month before my trip to introduce myself and to let agents and casting directors know when I was arriving. Also, I did not tell them that I only planned to be there about a month. How could an agent possibly represent someone who wasn't going to be around long enough for them to invest in? Agents are more inclined to consider you if you are going to stick around. In my cover letter I stated my arrival date and requested an opportunity to meet with them. I did not mention how long I planned to stay. Although I had a dated return ticket, I was open to the possibilities. Should I nab an agent who is willing to work for me, then that return flight would have definitely been returned.

I sent follow-up postcards about one week before my flight. Since I sent the initial mailing about a month prior, follow-up postcards closer to the date of arrival are good reminders that you will be in town in a matter of days. These offices may have expressed interest in your initial mailing, but may have put your picture aside knowing you are not in town yet. These follow up postcards help to refresh their memories of your initial mailing and your interest to meet with them. Hopefully it will spark their interest to meet with you too!

- **New Rezies** *for LA Market*

Although I am not completely knowledgeable on all the do's and don'ts of an LA headshot resume, here are some details that I worked on to gear my resume for the LA market. The main difference with the LA resume is that you must have your stats on them. In NY, unless you are a model, most headshot resumes do not require your measurements. For the LA resume, be sure to have your height, weight, hair color and eye color listed.

The other difference I found is that you should put film and television credits above theatre credits, regardless if your theatre credits are more substantial. NY is a huge theatre town and most of our work may be based on stage. However in LA, guest starring and principal roles in TV and film have more weight and are more impressive to an agent's eye. I also discovered that color headshots are very popular out there as well, but for my purposes, I stuck with the traditional black and white headshots.

Also be sure to list a local LA number as one of your contact numbers as well as any other additional numbers you want to add (see below).

- **Local Number**

I signed up for a local LA number because I felt that LA agents and casting directors would be more inclined to call if they saw a local number as opposed to calling long distance. If they see an LA number, I think they are more likely to assume you are serious about your stay. If they only see long distance numbers, they may assume you have no intention of making a serious commitment to LA. Whether or not that is the case, you want them to call you. It's also easier and cheaper for them to call a local number.

I had an extra cell phone that I wasn't using and I was able to hook up a local LA phone number. It was a prepaid national phone plan that you just add minutes to whenever you need it. This worked out very well for me. So choose an option that works for you, but definitely invest in a local number.

- **Car**

I rented a car out there for my stay. Here is where a good portion of my budget went. If you don't have access to a car, then this may be your only alternative, so save for it. Do your research and call all the rental agencies to compare prices. I spent about $500 total for my three week car rental including gas. Here are some other things I found out:

If you pick up and drop off at the airport, the rate is cheaper. I'm not sure if this is the case for all rental companies, but that is what I discovered when comparing prices.

If you own a platinum credit card, there may be auto insurance included. However their coverages may vary so be sure to inquire what the plan includes. Also, the credit card auto insurance only covers up to 14 days of consecutive rental. So if your stay is 30 days, you can't use your credit card insurance. So to get around that, I decided to make two different reservations with two different platinum cards so that I could break up the consecutive days and be eligible for the credit card auto insurance. I opted for this solution because signing up for auto insurance with the rental agencies would have doubled my expense. In hindsight I'm not sure if what I did using two different reservations under different cards would have been valid, but thankfully, I safely drove the streets of LA and the issue did not come up. Be sure to check around with your credit card companies to see what their auto insurance plans offer and what their restrictions may be.

- **Apartment**

If you don't have a friend you can stay with or a couch you can crash on, Craigslist is an amazing resource for shares and sublets, as well as many other topics. Just log onto www.craigslist.com and click on LA, then click on "Temporary/Sublets" or the category that best suits your needs. You can post a housing ad at no cost. You should start looking as soon as you buy your airline tickets so you can get a feel for what's available. A lot of the listings are for more immediate openings, but you'll find, at least I did, a good portion of the listings that will match your needs. Keep in mind also that a lot of the availability dates are at the start of the month, as in the 1st. So when deciding on your stay, maybe plan to arrive on earlier part of the month or as the month is ending as opposed to the middle.

I posted an ad stating the dates I was going to be in LA and how much I wanted to spend. I received great responses and was able to line up appointments to see the apartments right away. Ultimately I found a great one bedroom sublet with private parking. When you're looking for a place, try to find a place that has private parking. Finding street parking is insane in certain neighborhoods, especially with the street cleaning rules so having one less thing to worry about was very helpful for me. There are new listings everyday and many options in terms of studios, shares, length of stay, and neighborhoods.

On the topic of neighborhoods, I think Hollywood, North and West are very central. LA overall is extremely spread out but I found these locations to be in the heart of LA and a good place to start when looking for a place to live. If you love the beach, Santa Monica is a beautiful area, but it isn't the most convenient location in relation to its distance from Hollywood, where I think most auditions are held. But again, I can't stress enough how spread out LA is so auditions and studios can very well be all over town. I also stayed at a hotel in Century City for a weekend when my boyfriend was visiting and although I was only there for a weekend, it seemed more of a business district—think *LA Law* urban-type setting. What I liked about the Hollywood area was that is was close to the heart of Sunset Boulevard, Santa Monica Boulevard, and of course Hollywood Boulevard where there is a lot to see and do.

Overall, from what I've heard and what I've experienced, it is relatively easy to find housing in LA. A lot of that is because LA houses actors. "Making it" in Hollywood is tough so the swarm of actors flying into LA with the hope of fulfilling their dreams is equaled by the swarm of actors who leave in search of new ones. As such, the turnover of available apartments can be high. When I drove around LA, I constantly saw signs for available rentals and vacancies.

- **Reel/Demo**

In regards to a reel, I was lucky to have a friend who worked in television that offered to make a reel for me so it didn't cost me anything, except to buy the blank tapes and covers. I wanted to be as prepared as possible when I hit LA so that if an agent requested a reel, I'd have it.

On December 10, 2003 I went to a free Pilot Season seminar at Actors Connection in NYC which was very helpful as it addressed many of the issues and concerns I had about LA and the LA market. I learned that in LA, you almost always audition with sides so you don't have to worry so much about monologues the way we do here in NY. I also found out that there is no freelancing in LA. They may practice what is called "hip-pocketing," a form of freelancing, but it is rare. Other tips mentioned include not overlooking assistants for they may be the future agents and casting directors (this tip is good anywhere), that most LA offices are okay with drop-offs, and that you don't need an agent to go out to LA. If you have the opportunity to attend a Pilot Season seminar, especially if it's free, it is a great place to get some helpful advice for the trip and a great place to hear feedback from other actors' experiences with LA.

In regards to a reel, a lot of actors at the seminar who have been out to LA most often stated that a reel would be good to have in the event that an agent simply wanted to see what you looked like on film. I did not have a lot of material to put on a reel except for a couple of Indies, a makeover show and a commercial, but it was something more to offer in addition to a headshot. However, don't put a reel together just for the sake of having one—obviously make sure that it's something you are proud to show.

On the flip side, a lot of people at the seminar also stated not to spend a ton of money on making a reel until you need it, or basically until you are asked for one. Reels can be quite expensive and it is suggested that before you shell out the cash to have one made, be sure that it's not just going to sit on a shelf. If you find in your interviews that a lot of agents are asking you to provide one, then that's the time to think about preparing a reel. Until then, it may be best to save your money.

Now if you don't have anything to put on a reel, this is a non-issue. You may want to tell the agent that you are currently working to build your credits. I know that doesn't sound great, but it's an honest answer. This works best if you are just starting out or if most of your work has been on stage and you are just beginning to branch out into film and TV. Some actors suggested having a scene performed in class as something to put on a reel. I think that is risky, but if you're proud of the work, why not?

There are many different opinions on having a reel when you head West. Obviously the more you're armed with, the better, but ultimately that is something you'll decide based on your finances and your credits.

- **Extra Companies for Extra Cash!**

Since I did not have any immediate plans to get a "money" job out there outside of acting, I thought it would be a good idea to register with some extras casting companies. For one, it would provide me with extra cash and secondly, since my time was pretty much open, I thought it would be a great opportunity to see what the sets are like in LA.

There are several extras casting offices out in LA, but I think you only really need to register with Central Casting. If you look at the Ross Reports under Primetime shows, you'll see that the majority of extras are booked through Central Casting. Most of the extras agencies charge a registration fee of about $20 so this can add up. If you're in SAG, this fee is often waived, but there is sometimes a Polaroid fee of $2. Make sure you read the Ross Reports to determine which of these agencies charge a fee to join and how much. You'll also find that some of these offices have registration phone numbers that'll answer those questions as well as let you know if they have open calls. Central Casting does charge a $20 fee, regardless of Union affiliation, but for me that was worth it because as I said earlier, they do almost all of the background casting for Primetime shows. There are other offices like Bill Dance, The Casting Couch, Prime Casting, etc, but again call to find out about their registration requirements. Registering with too many offices can add up so my advice is to spend the $20 bucks on Central Casting and then perhaps register only with other agencies that do not charge a fee. This again goes back to how much money you have to spare.

An interesting thing I discovered when it came to Central Casting and perhaps the other extras agencies out in LA that you may not be aware of is that there is a "call-in" procedure. I was not aware of this. In NY, the casting offices for the most part call us when there is a booking for extra work. With Central Casting, they have a hotline number you call that has a recorded listing of all the parts they need to cast for background work. If you hear something that matches the type they are looking for, you call and state that you are available. You then hope that you are one of the first people that called to book the job. I guess in a sense, it is a race to make sure you check the recordings frequently, or hope that if you do fit a breakdown, they have the time to call you directly.

When I registered with Central Casting I met a woman who asked if I had a call-in service, and I mistakenly assumed she was asking if I had voicemail. I told her that I had voicemail but she explained that a call-in service was a service you hire to call those hotline numbers for you throughout the day. I guess that makes sense because if those recordings are constantly being updated, then you literally have to call as many times as possible to keep abreast of all the new castings. That can be very time consuming and costly so in LA they have these call-in agencies that monitor the calls for you. With the huge number of actors in LA, these extras casting offices don't really have the time to make all those individual calls to see who fits their needs and who is available. I'm not sure if all the extras agencies out there operate that way, but it was an interesting system. I know in NY, background casting offices such as Sylvia Fay and Grant Wilfley have a hotline number that is similar, but from my experience, most of the casting directors in NY, including Sylvia Fay and Grant Wilfley will call you directly if they have your picture on file and know you fit the breakdown. Personally, that's how I like it!

- **What to bring**

This is where I may not be the best person to ask because I truly tend to over pack, but I'll try to just list the essentials in no particular order of what was helpful for me:

1. Headshots—a fair amount depending on your length of stay. I packed about 100.
2. Cell Phone
3. Postcards (200)
4. Sized resumes (so you don't have to go to Kinko's to use the cutter)
5. Basic supplies—stapler, stapler remover, scissors, scotch tape, sharpies
6. 9X12 Envelopes (Optional—you can always grab more at Staples out there, plus less to weigh your luggage down)
7. Ross Reports

8. Sunglasses
9. Laptop
10. LA maps—especially the one that breaks it down to streets. *Thomas's Guide* is the most recommended as it breaks down maps from street to street.
11. Club or party clothes
12. Lt weight jacket—depending on when you go, it can get chilly at night
13. Nice interview outfits
14. Camera

Now that the prep work is done, here is how my journey to LA began. No one was more surprised than me to find out where it led . . .

Monday, December 22, 2003

I am very scared, nervous, excited, anxious, curious, and hopeful all rolled into one body that lately can't seem to stand or sit still. It's Pilot Season in LA and hit or miss, I am packing my bags! As I am writing this very paragraph it seems so overwhelming and even surreal that I have no idea what lies ahead. This is the first entry in my diary. I am very excited because in the past few weeks, I got some bites from my mailing!!! Woo Hoo!!!! I received a call from two casting directors and one agent who asked me to call them when I got to LA and one agency that said they'd call if they had something for me!!! It's a start! Every time my new cell phone rings, my heart does somersaults. I know it has to be a call from an LA agent or casting director because they are the only people who have that number from my mailings. I don't know what I will be writing in the days to come, but at the same time it is quite thrilling to embark on this quest. My flight to LA is not until January 9, but somehow I think my adventure has already begun.

Tuesday, January 6, 2004

Oh my gosh, I am going nuts. I thought I finalized my car situation, but today yet again, I found myself on the phone for hours figuring out the best course of action when it comes to transportation. I didn't realize that certain credit cards provided auto insurance so with that extra bit of knowledge, I rethought my rental situation. After all the research, it turns out that insurance is only covered if you rent no more than 14 consecutive days. My trip is longer than that. After speaking to one of the rental agencies, getting insurance from them will double my total! The credit card insurance only covers damage to the rental car and does not include liability (injury/damage to second party). That could get crazy. I don't plan on getting into any accidents, but I haven't driven in almost ten years! All this insurance lingo confused the crap out of me and so, true to form, I ended up making four different reservations!!! Ay ya yay! Guess I'll figure out which one works best for me when I get there. I'm a safety girl so I like to have back-ups for my back-ups.

Wednesday, January 7, 2004

Well, I have one more day before the big day. I am freaking out!!! I haven't been really nervous until today. For some reason, it hit me and it hit me HARD. I know for some, this may not be a big deal, but shipping out to LA is a huge deal for me. I am walking into the unknown and I am starting to feel it. I got an e-mail today from a potential roommate and it fell through because he found someone sooner. That really upset me. I guess because it seemed that everything else was falling into place, that bit of news made me realize that I head into unchartered, uncertain territories. My last day of work was Monday and that was very emotional as that officially marked my "jump" or I'd say leap—leap of faith. I've been packing the past few days and I am overwhelmed, mostly with all that I am bringing. I know I can probably minimize, but hey, I'm a chic, there are necessities. So that's where I find myself today—IN A PANIC! I almost feel like I can't breathe.

Friday, January 9, 2004

FLIGHT TO LA!
"Don't let anything get in the way of your destiny." That was a quote from the movie, *A View from the Top* starring Gwyneth Paltrow. I remember it because I saw this movie back in November when I was first considering this trip. In a way I give it some credit for inspiring me to go for it. Well, guess what!!!! That was the in flight movie!!!! I've been so nervous and anxious about this trip that when I heard that was the movie, it made me think that maybe that was some sort message for me, that I was heading in the right direction. In any event it made me hopeful and I started to get excited . . . .

Monday, January 12, 2004

What can I say about my first weekend here? To sum it up: SCARY. I have been a basket case these past couple of days. I was a total bitch to my boyfriend, Brad. He was so sweet to come with me to help me get settled this weekend and we spent most of it arguing. The cause: DRIVING. You have to understand, I haven't driven in over ten years and the thought of it literally petrifies me. But LA is a city of drivers. That is a cold hard fact. Well perhaps I could take the bus, but the bus system here is not like New York. Trust me, it isn't. I took a ride today and granted it wasn't horrible, and if you must opt for the bus, you will somehow get by, but I think if you take this route in LA, you must be prepared to spend a lot of time on the bus and a lot of time waiting for the bus. Anyhow, my boyfriend and I drove like fiends this whole weekend—a foreign feeling to us New Yorkers who are used to surviving mass transit. We hardly had anytime to really enjoy ourselves as I was too busy stressing the driving. Most people will not have the anxieties that I have had over the past few days. Every day this past weekend was such an emotional roller coaster. I feel so bad that my man and I had so much tension just because I lack driving skills. I even drove him to start smoking during our trip as my stress rubbed off on him, not to mention the near close collisions we had in the car, hee, hee. I laugh about it now, but believe me I wasn't laughing in the car, and neither was my boyfriend. I will be forever indebted to him for putting up with me.

So today was my first day driving by myself as Brad headed back to New York this morning. I was shaking like a leaf. I prayed all the way through. I was driving from the airport to my friend Donna's apartment in West Hollywood. That was a haul coming from the airport as I took the side streets and avoided the freeways like the plague. I think if you're creative, you can get almost anywhere in LA without driving on the freeways. At least, that's my plan. Anyway, I must not have breathed the whole ride. By the grace of God, I made it and found parking to boot! That I must say was very exciting. I felt liberated, for now. Well not exactly my first ideal weekend here in LA, but it made me realize that I need to toughen up as this is a new city to me with new ways of doing things. There were many times where I was on the verge of tears. I feel alone out here and I have to learn everything by myself. The thought is so daunting to me. You know, if I didn't have to drive, I know I'd be 100 times more confident about this adventure. I will do my best to face the challenge. I am scared and worried about the other challenges that may lie ahead. To be honest, I feel so overwhelmed right now.

So here I am, by myself trying to relax. When I was in NY planning my living arrangements, I spoke to my friend Donna in LA who said she was going to Salt Lake City for a couple of days and offered to let me stay at her apartment while she was away. I originally had a hotel booked for my stay but that was going to cost me a pretty penny so when Donna offered to let me stay at her place, I quickly decided to cancel my hotel reservations and save some money. I don't know what I was thinking booking a hotel, but at the time I figured it was my only choice. Luckily Donna offered a solution for a couple of days. Since I still had to think about a place to live for the rest of my stay, I began to search through Craigslist (best non-fee source) for temporary housing opportunities. I should have done that from the beginning. I must have corresponded with at least 20 people. It was hard doing that from New York because most people wanted to show the place right away and it's hard when you're not there yet, obviously. So I ended up missing out on a lot of places. But that's why I monitored the site every hour on the hour when I could. I'm a maniac like that. I saw several places, but the main downside for me was that there was only street parking. Trust me, out here you want to find a place that has private parking, especially if you're not comfortable driving. Street parking is so tough here and they have street cleaning rules on certain days so you can't park in certain areas during those designated times and yada, yada, yada. It's been a *very* long time since I needed to pay attention to parking rules and regulations so I was very nervous and almost compulsive about checking the signs even after I already parked. If you're like me when it comes to driving, place an ad on craigslist that inquires about private parking/garage availability—that is KEY. I saw a place this evening that looks great and it would be my own place for the next three weeks. I'm scheduled to pay tomorrow and will touch base on how that develops. The other places I saw were shares with no private parking so this other place won hands down. I thought about wanting to live with someone just for the company, but in the end having my own private space was more important to me. If all goes well with this place, I could move in tomorrow! I know I still have Donna's place for the next day, but I really want to just get settled and unpacked.

Tuesday, January 13, 2004

I'm home!!! When I was reading all these books on how to prepare for LA, nothing could be truer than when they said you can't begin to focus on finding acting work until you have a place to live. Well that is for damn sure! If you take only one thing from this journal, take that. Since I had Donna's apartment for only 2 days, I didn't bother to completely unpack. I couldn't relax or even start thinking about calling casting directors or going on registrations until I was settled somewhere. For all of you making the trip, give yourself at least one week just to settle in. It's important to plan your length of stay with that consideration.

Right now I feel like I'm in a foreign country rather than just on the West Coast. It is as if I'm learning everything all over again. Sometimes even a simple trip to the market has an air of unfamiliarity here. There is this constant feeling that I need to ask for directions or permission to do something. I know that sounds silly, but I keep thinking that maybe they do things a lot differently here than they do in NYC. I didn't want to feel and especially, look like an idiot. So a lot of things for me, even a simple trip to the store today were done with some hesitancy.

So as I was saying, you can't do ANYTHING until you have a place to live. That is muy importante. With that said, I finally have my clothes in a closet and my suitcases put away. Whew! That was an exhausting process. It is no fun living out of a suitcase. I feel, as do my clothes, like I can now breathe. And boy can they ever. Through the grace of God, I found a beautiful place. The woman who lives here, Colette is traveling to San Francisco on business so I have the place to myself. It is a bright, sun filled, clean and very organized one bedroom with an airy living room and large terrace past Beachwood Canyon in Hollywood. It has a private parking slot!!!!!!!!! I cannot tell you how fucking fantastic that is, especially based on my dramas with driving! It is in a residential neighborhood and in an elevator building with laundry facilities. The location is perfect as it has shops, restaurants, and a large grocery store all within walking distance. I couldn't ask for more and the best part about it is the rent—only $600! This place is HUGE! I can't even imagine how much a place like this would go for in NYC. Wow, to think that I was going to pay almost 1000 dollars to stay at a hotel with no kitchen, no terrace, and no coziness. Here, I was living in a home. All I know is that she is living pretty and I am grateful that my pickyness led me to this apartment. Colette is also in the entertainment business but behind the camera. She is very nice and trusting, as I guess, I have been. We literally just met yesterday. She showed me around this beautiful spacious apartment and without hesitation I said, "I'll take it!" and without the slightest hesitation, she said "Great!" To us New Yorkers who know what it's like to live in closet-sized apartments, space is a beautiful thing. I really didn't get to know her much and she didn't even ask me for references. On that thought, I should have asked her for references. We just basically relied on trust, but I did have her sign an agreement/receipt verifying that I paid her the full sublease amount and the deposit. At the very least, if there is no formal or even informal contract, make sure you have the person sign something that says you paid for the length of your stay and be sure to include contact names and phone numbers for precaution.

In essence, it can happen that fast here in LA. Finding a place to live can get crazy, but in LA it is much easier. It is just a matter of finding what's right and important for you—whether it's a private place or a share, distance to shops, parking availability, etc. I know I was a bit picky, but have no fear that you will find tons of listings on Craigslist. Even just driving around you'll see tons of vacancy signs. It is after all, LA—actor central. Finding a place in LA can happen in a NY minute.

So here I am, settled in finally, not knowing what to do with myself. I will cook dinner for myself tonight so that should keep me busy. I also have to plan my wardrobe for tomorrow for my first appointment. I will be registering with LA Casting, an extras casting company, so hopefully I can make a little money while I am here. I have also finally started calling the two casting directors and the agent that responded to my mailing. I know that probably should have been the first thing I did when I arrived, but like I said, I couldn't even focus on setting up any meetings until I was unpacked and settled.

Now the problem with setting up some of these appointments is that in LA, everything is so sppppprrrrrrrreeeeeeeeaaaaaaad out. Based on traffic and location, it's hard to gauge how much time to leave in between appointments with enough time to travel from one place to the other. There is a lot of traffic out here. Since I am new, without much sense of distances from location to location, it's hard for me to map out when I should make these appointments. Right now I'm hoping to do one appointment a day so that I am not racing around all of LA and believe me, these casting directors and agents are all over the place—sometimes within one to two hours of each other by car! It's true! This is so strange to me because in NY you can get pretty much anywhere for auditions within a half-hour so you can feasibly arrange to go on four or five auditions a day without breaking a sweat. Granted these are just perceptions for now, but I did map out where some of these offices are and for example, if I made one appointment on 3rd street and Bixel and I had another interview say in Encino—which I actually do, if I make these appointments the same day, I have to give myself an extra two and a half hours to get from one place to the next—at least. So with that in mind, appointments have to be strategized based on locations. You want to be relaxed enough when you drive so that when you get there, you are at your best, and not rushing to leave to make your next appointment. I can bet it is very easy for someone to sense that "rushing" vibe. So it is best to schedule appointments with enough time to get there and enough time to have a relaxed interview. I guess we'll see if I can manage that.

Wednesday, January 14, 2004

Well what started out as an uneventful day turned out to be quite heart-racing for me. This morning I registered with an extras casting company to hopefully book some work for extra cash. Thankfully that went pretty smoothly. I drove and got there just fine. I went back home for lunch and debated whether or not to attend this open call at the Roosevelt Hotel on Hollywood Boulevard. My first instincts were not to go as it didn't sound very legit. With all my experience with scams in NY you'd think I'd trust my same instincts here, but no, I made myself go, mainly with several thoughts:

1. I didn't have any other plans
2. To force myself to drive
3. To get out there and look for opportunities
4. To force myself to drive

Well, let's just say I should have trusted my instincts. I drove there and found first, that Hollywood Boulevard was closed off due to a movie premier—I should have known! There's a premier here almost every day—exciting, yes, convenient, no. So I had to take an alternate route which freaked me out because I like to map things out before I get behind the wheel. So instead, I had to cautiously find an alternate route that would not get me lost or worse, get me in an accident. I ended up finding parking for $8 which to LA standards, I guess is a lot. I didn't care, I was just happy to park. So I walk to the Roosevelt Hotel and speak to the Concierge regarding this open call. He's like, "Oh man, I should have brought my headshots." I was like, Sheesh! Everyone here really is an actor. I go on to tell him a bit more about it and he seems skeptical and tells me he's been to similar "open calls" with so called "talent scouts" and in the end, all they wanted was your cold hard cash. DUH! I know this. What am I doing here??? I called my friend Michael and he too agreed that it sounded shady. Instincts. Ya gotta trust 'em. So I made the decision to leave. I know, I was already there, why not check it out? After all, I couldn't be sure if it was legitimate or not. Well, I wasn't going to ignore my instincts a second time. I figured any legitimate acting gig more so than not, would come from a casting director through an audition, not this random meet-and-greet where you don't even need headshots. That alone should have made me reevaluate the call. Any job worth me getting behind the wheel is going to require that you at least have professional pictures. The other reason I decided to leave was that it was getting dark out and I try to avoid night driving as much as possible. What can I say, driving is not under my "Special Skills" category, but I can sure belly dance!

So I'm walking back on Hollywood Boulevard and I keep walking totally forgetting where I parked. The blocks get progressively seedier, and I mean five levels, sublevels, below port authority on a very bad night. So I start to feel the first waves of panic. Uh oh, am I lost? Hawthorne Street, I know that's where I parked. Where the fuck is it?? I somehow proceed to walk even further east knowing I must have passed that street already. Somehow my feet aren't listening to my gut—which was strongly telling me to turn around and GET OUT! Scary looking people start coming out now, various outbursts here and there, random yelling as I try to ignore the "undesirables." I notice a group behind me causing a raucous so I quicken my pace to create a distance, almost on the verge of tears. I start to pray. Another leer, help. I finally decide to turn back, past the same leery fella who probably thought I turned around to get some—yeah, right. So I move past him trying to ignore the hint of recognition on his face. How did I get this far out of the way??? Funny, why is it when we know we should turn back we keep walking in the same wrong direction?

Anyway, remember that rowdy group I was talking about? Turns out that they were getting arrested! Just great. I see cops putting them in handcuffs as I walk past them thinking . . . shit, this group was walking right behind me only minutes ago. I wonder what they did? Actually, ignorance is bliss. So, the sun was starting to go down and if I didn't hurry up and find my car, so was I. I get the nerve and approach one of the officers surrounding this motley bunch of criminals. Probably a bad idea in case a shooting occurs, but I stop anyway and ask one of the police officers for directions to Hawthorne Street. I mean, who better to ask, surely not my admirer a block back. She points me in the right direction and I start to relax, but not before I hightailed it away from this arrest area. Freakin' Hawthorne Street! Boy did I ever walk *way* past it. First of all, the streets in LA have a gazillion names. Hawthorne was the block where I parked, but for some reason, the street name somehow changed *within* that same block! What is that?! Okay, in all fairness I guess an LA native would say the same about the Village in NYC. Anyway, that was my little field trip to Hollywood. SO not glamourous. Lesson for the day: TRUST YOUR INSTINCTS!!! Especially if you're new to a city.

Thursday, January 15, 2004

I am so pissed!!! Today I went to Central Casting in Burbank to register as it is one of the biggest extras casting company in LA. Well, when my boyfriend Brad and I previously tried to map out the route, we couldn't find it. I thought I printed it out on MapQuest but I guess I didn't so it was totally my fault. Everyone I talked to said it was very tricky to get to, especially if you're not familiar with the roads so rather than stress it out driving on my own with the likelihood of getting lost, I decided to shell out the cash and take a cab. Big mistake. Oh my gosh! It was the easiest route ever!!! What a waste of money. I paid $23 to get there and another $20 to get back home!!! I felt like such a ding, ding. As I watched the driver and the route, it couldn't have been any easier. Take it from me, taking cabs in LA is not the way to go unless you have the cash to throw.

Before I called a cab to take me back home, I was told there was a Metrolink train just down the block. Thinking I could save $20, I walked over there to check it out. Oy! There was no one there and I couldn't even understand the transit maps. I got the metrolink confused with the metrorail—which I'm kind of familiar with based on the information I researched online. I used the passenger information phone and spoke with a representative who sort of walked me through the trains that I had to take to get me back to Hollywood. Turns out that I had to take the Metrolink to Union Station, and then transfer to the Metrorail to take me to Hollywood—that's if I understood him correctly. Sounds simple enough. Well, unfortunately, the next train wasn't for another hour and a half! It was hot and I was so frustrated with it all that I decided to walk back to Central Casting and call a cab. Well not all cabs pick up in Burbank so I called a different cab company that sounded a bit shady on the phone. The cab company I took to Burbank was great but they don't service Burbank so I got stuck with this other one not knowing what other companies to call. The cab finally arrives with no distinguishing names or logos on the car. Two women walk out of the Central Casting and one of them stops and says, "That's a cab company?" and wished me luck with some looks of apprehension. That wasn't very comforting but at this point I wanted to get home so I was like, screw it. Probably not the best thing I could have done. If I have to, I can scream until all hell breaks loose so they better not mess with me. I get in the car where there are two men who barely speak English asking me where to go. I give them the address and get this, they're like, "Excuse me miss, but how do you get there?" Are you kidding me?! You are the cab company! It's your job to know!!!!! I literally had to navigate him every road—ME giving them directions and I'm not even from here! I was so over this. Thankfully, I knew the way home. Geez! Where's the 6 train when you need it!

On the positive side, I met a wonderful woman while I was registering who was extremely helpful in terms of giving me information on SAG and their LA offices. She even offered to drive me back to Hollywood, but she wasn't going in that direction. Boy, do I wish she did!!

In LA, if you don't have wheels, expect to shell out quite a bit of money on cabs. LA is very spread out so if you choose this method of transportation, expect your cash to run out pretty quickly. Buses are another option, but they do not travel as frequently as they do in NY, some of them perhaps only once every hour. On the upside, a bus ride can cost as low as 25 cents! As far as the trains go, let's just say, they *don't*. LA's Metrorail Red Line, albeit impeccably clean, is very limited to just certain central areas of LA so it will not get you everywhere. One day, I ventured underground during rush hour down the Hollywood Station and it was like a ghost town. Cut to Times Square Station at the witching hour and you can gather a crowd fit for a concert. What I'm trying to say is that everyone in LA drives. Forget mass transit.

Tuesday, January 20, 2004

Big day today! I "took my first meeting" here with an LA agent, one of the industry people that responded to my mailing! I left messages last week with the casting directors who also responded, but I have yet to hear from them. In the meantime, I am taking a meeting with an agent!! In LA, that's what they say, "take meetings." I told my friend Donna about this agency and although she's never heard of them, she said to take what I can get as it is Pilot Season here. So off I went. My appointment was for 1:30. When I got there, the person I was meeting with hadn't arrived yet as I was early (as usual). Walking into this small office there were stacks and stacks of headshots on the tables, the floor, everywhere! I couldn't believe it. Welcome to LA. Actually, it's probably the same in NY. It is quite unbelievable how many headshots come through an agency's door. I was glad that mine somehow managed to stand out for a meeting. That made me feel pretty good and I started to relax.

The agent arrived and he was a very friendly Asian man. Interestingly enough, his entire staff (of about three people) was all Asian people.

So, I relaxed a bit more. I figured, hey, I'm one of their peeps. I filled out some talent forms and by the way, when asked to do this, be sure to check both sides. The assistant who handed it to me didn't mention there were 2 sides so when asked if I was done, I said yes. He noticed the form wasn't complete so I had to finish the other side, a bit embarrassing as I wanted to make a good impression. While waiting for the interview to begin, I heard the agent on the phone talking to a casting director for upcoming submissions and I realized this was the real deal and so I started getting nervous.

After my forms were complete, he asked me into his office and we chatted about me being in LA and if I had moved here permanently. I said yes because I figured no agent would represent someone who was here only temporarily or on a "feeler" trip, as I was. So I thought it best to increase my odds and say I was settling in here. The rest of the conversation went as I expected; what do you want to do here in LA, what work have you done, what work won't you do, etc., basically typical interview questions. There was nothing that was going make me stand out and as I sensed we were about to wrap up our conversation and not wanting to leave on a flat note, I decided to share a little story about my experiences in LA. I told him that my sister gave me a camcorder for Christmas and that I was documenting this trip to show to my friends who are thinking about heading to LA. His interest was piqued and I could tell he was finding me more interesting. He said that I was already thinking about directing which we laughed about. I told him how I hadn't driven in over ten years and that I had such dramas simply getting gas and that Brad, my boyfriend caught this all on video. I don't think it was my imagination, but as I continued recounting my LA adventures, I could tell he saw more and more to me. Afterwards, he even said that I had a great personality and that I was very bubbly with great energy. This is where I truly believed that my interview shifted. I was no longer just another aspiring actress walking through his door, but instead, my personality showed him that I was a real person and that I was fun! Whether or not he takes me on as a client, I know that I made a positive impression and left on an even more positive note. He said he'll take a look at my demo and see what he can do for me. Sounds good to me!

From this interview I learned a very important lesson when it comes to meeting with agents and casting directors. These people see actors all the time. Even though training and previous work are definitely important, I think what ultimately will make the difference is personality. So don't be afraid to be yourself and share a bit of who you are to them. If I hadn't mentioned a funny personal experience, I probably would have been just another picture in his stack, but because I shared a little bit of myself with him—non-acting related—I was able to make a difference. There was a person he liked behind the picture.

Wednesday, January 21, 2004

I don't have any appointments scheduled for the day so I am spending a lot of time on the internet. One of the sites I like to check out is *Backstage's* Chat Room. For all those who are not familiar with this, it is a site (www.backstage.com) where actors can find castings, articles and a chat room where they can voice their opinions on absolutely anything. You can ask questions, get feedback, etc. It is really great and it is free. Well a few days ago I posted a topic regarding "Getting Invited to LA." I was curious about how other actors felt about that. I got a lot of interesting feedback on both sides. Some said you can't wait forever to be invited and others said many established actors got their start in NY and eventually made it to LA because they booked a job. One respondent really hit it home.

Before I go into his response, I want to say that the reason I posted that topic is because I was having second thoughts about being here in LA without any real solid leads. I read various articles and watched interviews where many actors waited until they booked work out here before they made the big move. There is also the fact that almost everything in film and TV is taped out here in LA. On the other hand, there are also more actors out here who compete for those parts. How do you weigh all these factors and decide where to be?

In light of all that, one response to my posting really affected me. He basically stated that your surroundings don't make you successful. YOU make things happen in whatever surroundings you are in. In other words, you have to believe that it doesn't matter so much where a person pursues his craft, but instead what matters is what the person does with the surroundings he's in. Ultimately he said to choose a place where you feel you are going to thrive. That bit of advice made me feel so much better. I realized that I put so much pressure on myself being here in LA and making things happen when I should really start focusing on where I feel I can best be productive. It is an issue I need to explore more while I am here.

To make things even more frustrating, in the time that I have been here, I have so far, been called several times for work in NY!!!! How crazy is that?!! When I get these calls, I start getting impatient for my return flight! But I know that I have to give this place the shot it deserves so I settle myself by getting my mind back in that focus.

A huge part of me also has this need to make the people back in NY proud. So many people know that I am here and wishing me well. I get scared that I am going to disappoint them if I return. That's such a big part of who I am—the need to please. I know I shouldn't care what anyone else thinks, but when you're in this business so many people expect you to fail or more to the point, don't expect you to succeed. Because of that, you want so desperately to prove them wrong.

Saturday, January 24, 2004

Oh what a night! Brad is here for the weekend and we had plans to check out the LA nightlife. I figured this trip to LA would not be complete without a stop at one of LA's hot spots. So tonight we went to dine at Asia de Cuba in LA's posh Mondrian Hotel. We got all dolled up and I was very excited to be part of the LA scene. Plus I just bought these fabulous shoes that were so pointy they could pick a lock. I chose Asia de Cuba on the recommendation of several friends, as well as Access Hollywood, my entertainment superhighway. I remember many times where they featured the Mondrian and Sky Bar as one of LA's "it" spots, so off we went.

We arrived and walked in to this simply beautifully designed hotel, with the hotel staff in what appeared to be soft linen suits. The word "clean" comes to mind—and I ain't talking Ajax, but clean in the sense of style. It is like the feeling when you wake up with the sun shining and you open the veranda doors to welcome the ocean breeze. That's what it felt like to me. At nighttime it was pure elegance. Brad and I proceeded to the bar, where else, and ordered ourselves some tropical looking martinis to complete our look for the evening. The crowd was mixed—you had your sexy twenty-somethings, distinguished forty-somethings, even a celeb siting (James Caan, if not a very close look-a-like at the bar) and a bit of everything in between,—all well-dressed and having a most *divine* time, dahling. That seemed to be the mood of every moment here. While we waited for our table, with martinis in hand, we took a tour around and were recommended to check out the view from the patio area. So we stepped out into this area and a few steps up there was a dimly lit pool and surrounding the pool were these beds—yes indeed—beds with heat lamps over them! On these beds, the trendiest of the Hollywood circle mingle and lounge as they sip their colorful cocktails and 'tinis. So what is there to do but join them. Brad and I spotted an empty bed and plopped our New York asses down amused at the "chic-ness" of it all. From these beds a spectacular view of LA is at your feet and literally too—if you happen to be sprawled on the bed. It was quite a scene to behold. As Carrie Bradshaw would say, "I have to wonder, is this scene really what LA is all about? Schmooze and Booze, See and Be Seen?" I kept fantasizing about how many deals were being made at these tables, how many actors and actresses were here looking to catch the eye of a famous director, how many screenwriters were here celebrating their first successful pitch. It was the first time during this trip that my perception of LA glam was feeling like reality. Here, in this place, I was taking it all in.

After waiting an extra 30 minutes for our table, we were finally seated for dinner . . . and it was well worth the wait. We had a wonderful waitress and the food was absolutely fantastic. Everything we had was perfection from the calamari salad to the barbeque salmon, mmmmmmmm, my taste buds were loving me. After we had dinner, we had plans to check out the famed Sky bar, but alas, it was roped off for a private party. I wondered what Hollywood mogul was throwing a bash this night? It was after all, the night before the Golden Globes. Thinking our invitations to this exclusive party must have gotten lost, we decided to call it a night. Whereas in NYC heading home is done by the mere hail of a cab, here, we at the lobby, were greeted by a circle of people waiting for their cars—oh, excuse me, luxury vehicles. Valet, baby—the culture of LA. We waited about 20 minutes more before our four-door Ford rental pulled up. Yep, an impeccable standout to the silver Mercedes to our front and the red Ferrari to our back. We were travelin' in style!

On the ride home I asked myself if I could get used to this "scene" of fast cars and fancy parties. The answer: ABSOLUTELY. Now please understand that I don't have to live this lifestyle everyday but it sure is nice to have the option, and more especially, it would be nice to have the *means*.

Wednesday, January 28, 2004

Well it is my last week here and three more days until I head back to NYC. I am very anxious to get back. My feelings about this trip are very mixed at this point. I haven't heard back from the agent I met with and never got called back by the casting directors who initially expressed interest. Yes, I went in with the attitude of "hopeful, but realistic," but there was definitely a part of me that was hoping to wow the city, hoping to get that big break. I think a lot of actors head to LA with that thought in mind. I have only been in LA for three weeks and most actors are here for years hoping and wishing for their chance at Hollywood stardom. I've learned that three weeks is not enough time to establish relations here, much less book work. That is for sure. Most people spend years constantly working at that.

As I sit here thinking if I could have done more to get work or make contacts, I realize that this is a business of waves and cycles. You have to be willing to invest the time and see where the waves take you. The big question then becomes *where* do you want to invest the time.

So here again I find myself at this crossroad: LA to the left, NY to the right. Which way to go? For those of you who have never used *Backstage's* Online Chat room, as I mentioned earlier, it is basically an open forum where actors can post topics on everything and anything that they wish to address. I've always found it to be a great source for opinions and advice from my peers. Oftentimes, it can also be a great support system. So through this source, I recently enlisted the aid of my fellow actors and here are some responses to this neverending debate:

BACKSTAGE POSTING: GP (that's me)
To protect identities, I have changed the names of the respondents.

GP: I have often heard that it is best to move to LA only if "invited" there by an agent and/or invited for a particular project, film, TV, etc. I've heard that although most everything is taped out in LA, it is harder to get work because of the numbers who swarm there for that reason.

How much truth is there to these statements? I totally get that you can't *not* do something or go somewhere because someone tells you not to. You have to find out for yourself. However, the reason I ask this question is that in recent interviews I've read and watched, a lot of actors didn't make the big move out to LA until they were "asked" to do either a sitcom or movie, etc.

In light of that, do most people in LA find that getting work is easier because there are more opportunities out there OR do you find that it is harder to get work because there are more actors who go there, increasing the numbers game??

LS: What if you're not invited? Ever? Still going to wait?

JP: Hey GP, before I give you my opinion I want you to know that I am one who is sick and tired of being sick and tired of LA. So my thoughts and experiences here are negative, but don't let it discourage you because it is "one man's opinion."

So if you heard "it is harder to get work out here because of the numbers who swarm here for that reason" you have no idea how true it is. That's the main reason why I got sick of it here. Not only almost EVERYONE here wants to be an actor even non-actors want to be actors and a lot of them are just after the fame fantasy. I want to be surrounded by true artists rather than wanna-be's. Not only that, the social life is really dry here. I'm not saying there is no social life but I guess it's something only New Yorkers and Europeans will understand. Driving . . . I hate it! Traffic is insane here. Everything is far. Like yourself, since I established some contacts with casting directors and filmmakers I was afraid to move away but the truth is that MOST actors started in NY and work brought them here. From all I know and the research I've done, NY is where actors starve for a passion and LA is where actors starve for a fantasy. Now don't get me wrong there are a few lucky ones who start here and grow here. But just like you said GP, "I totally get that you can't not do something or go some where because someone tells you not to. You have to find out for yourself." That is so very true. I guess in a couple of months I will feel in NY what you feel here.

NE: Well, that is definitely one opinion on the matter. I guess it is good to hear both sides of the coin when you are just starting out, however you must choose on what is sound advice and just plain negativity.

Honestly, where is it posted that MOST actors come from NEW YORK?

Listen, whether you are in LA or NY the surrounding should not make one bit of difference on your career taking off. If you feel this is what you want then you can make it happen anywhere. AND YOU MUST BELIEVE THAT ABOUT YOURSELF.

There is not one right absolute place over another—it is solely based on preference and how comfortable you feel. If you have the drive and desire to compete and learn then you make your surrounding happen for you—not the other way around.

BOTTOM LINE—Welcome to LA. Get some training behind you, make some contacts, be professional, and never lose focus. One week can turn into months if you are not careful.

GP: Thanks to JP and NE. I really appreciate your thoughts on both sides of the coin. I think NE brought up a great point that you have to find the place where you are comfortable and can thrive. "Make your surroundings happen for you." Best advice I've heard. So I guess time will tell where I feel I can be most productive. I am new to LA so I am still overwhelmed—the driving is what stresses me the most and that's the VERY LAST thing that I should be concerned about as an actress. Heck, that shouldn't even be a factor, but it is for me so perhaps NY is a better fit.

But I am not one to give up so easily so I am going to give it a shot here. But it is good to hear that whether one chooses to pursue their craft in LA or NY, what matters is not location, but the person and their drive.

NINE: Thanks guys for all of your helpful feedback. I'm just curious... what is the driving like. I know it's HORRIBLE, but can you go on mapquest.com and type in two addresses and it tells you how long it takes to get from point A to point B... going the speed limit? How long, with traffic, would it take to get into and out of LA if say you lived up in the Hollywood Hills or West Hollywood?

VED: Ha, ha, ha. That is funny. Add an hour to the time and you've got it.

GP: Well you're asking someone who avoids the freeways like the plague. As I said I've been here about a week and have only traveled along the Blvds, e.g., Santa Monica, Cuengha, La Cienega, etc.

But yes, mapquest will give you the APPROX time. If you throw in traffic, you may, as VED suggested, have to tack on an extra 30-60 minutes. What I do is, I enter the "to" and "from" addresses in mapquest and it gives me the directions. HOWEVER, most of these directions use the freeways and highways. I adjust the directions and find an alternate route where I do not have to go on the freeways. So for me, I add even more time so I am not late.

It hasn't been so horrible yet. For example, I needed to get from Tamarind Ave by Franklin Ave to 10835 Santa Monica Blvd. Rather than taking the freeway, I took Santa Monica Blvd all the way down. I left at 11:30AM and got there at 12:15 (with some minor traffic included), so about 45 minutes and that was a simple route. So from North Hollywood to West LA perhaps 45minutes-1.5 hours, I'm guessing, unless there's traffic.

Hope this helps!

AG: The traffic in LA is bad, I won't lie about that. If you want an idea go to *http://www.sigalert.com/AlertInfo.asp?Region=Greater+Los+Angeles&auto=1*

And click on MAPs. It shows you a map of LA freeways with traffic. With some planning though, it's all do-able. LA veterans rarely are late because of traffic.

JP I don't know who you've been meeting in LA but I've met many actors who love working and don't care an ounce about fame. I'm sure there are just as many fame seekers in NY as in LA. It's true, we do have a lot of non-actors saying they want to be actors, but that's all they're doing. I can say I want to be a professional skateboarder, but I'm not doing anything about it. Doesn't make me a skateboarder at all, just makes me someone who likes to talk a lot.

MOST actors don't start in NY and move their way over when they're "invited." MOST actors aren't invited anywhere. Most working actors busted their butts to get where they are and didn't wait for anyone's permission.

NE: That is why the Valley or North Hollywood is a good place to live. You have all the necessities of stores around you and can avoid driving on the freeways for very long. Once you live here a bit you can figure out when traffic gets hectic and which roads are better to take at certain times. Traffic is not that bad if you understand it.

QT: GP, here's the reality of LA—even if you do come here because someone "invited" you, chances are that when you show up at the party you won't actually be on the guest list. I know sooooooooo many actors who came to LA because the west coast chapter of their NYC agency just LOVED them—and you know what? They are in the same boat as the rest of us—starting from scratch. Why? Because so and so left the agency, or not everyone in the west coast office liked them, or whatever. Yes, a lot of people in NYC tell you not to move to LA until you have lots and lots of NY credits, but the reality is that most LA people could care less about credits from NY. Unless you're being invited here because you are already a movie star, you're not really being invited. I know what agents and casting directors SAY, but I also know the reality of LIFE and WORKING in LA. Now that you are an Angelino the most important lesson you can learn is to take EVERY SINGLE THING SOMEONE IN THE INDUSTRY TELLS YOU WITH A GRAIN OF SALT.

JP: Not all actors are fame seekers, I know a few actors who are all about the art. I think what I was trying to say was that from seeing sooooooooo many (I think almost everybody in LA) people who want to be actors and a lot of them are not serious about it as I am (and of course many others) it just makes it look more like a la-la land if you know what I mean. I want to be surrounded by many people who are really about the art and craft of acting. I don't know if I make any sense to you but I hope you got my point. And about the wanna-be skateboarder and just talking about it, well of course it doesn't make you one, but if you are trying to do it and surrounded by people who just talk about it, I think you will get to a point where you are sick of it and need to change the environment. Anyway I think I confused myself here and am talking out of my ass. I better shut up and hear your thoughts people.

AG: I guess it's who you choose to surround yourself with. I've been out in LA long enough (and mostly not as an actor) and have lots of friends who have no interest in acting whatsoever. I also have friends who are very dedicated actors. I've met plenty of people who just want to be stars, but they're not my friends and I don't hang out with them.

Choose your group of friends and associates. You choose if you want to hang around people who drive around with their headshots pasted to the outside of their car, hoping someone will notice them. I don't and it doesn't bother me in the least that they're out there. Every city in the world is full of dreamers, LA is no exception.

SE: I think the most important thing is to establish yourself wherever you think you have the best chance of being personally happy. If you're already established in NYC and you're happy there, then stay. If you aren't happy there, then give LA a try.

Something like driving/traffic SHOULD be a consideration if it really bothers you. As well as smog and no weather (I'm from New England and going months without rain bugs the shit out of me, while to many other people, it's paradise) and whether it's too far from/too close to family. You have to take all these personal considerations into the equation, because they'll affect the long term viability of your ability to live and succeed in LA, regardless of how the acting career goes.

If you like NY, but want to do film and TV so you think you should come to LA, then try to build up some NY film/TV credits with those connections you already have. Once you have yourself a good reel with substantial credits, you'll know if NY has enough to offer you, or if it's really time to move to LA.

I agree with everyone else: if you wait to be invited, you'll be waiting a long time. The point behind those actors' stories who were invited is that they did good work and got noticed wherever they happened to be—NY, Australia, London—and their careers grew and naturally brought them to LA. If they'd come to LA first, they would have done the same work here that they did elsewhere to get themselves started.

LA is hard. I did the Big Move straight out of college not knowing a person in the city, no job, no place to live, and very little money. I'm glad I did it, but I see nothing wrong with taking advantage of the opportunities where you are already comfortable first.

It's important to accept that for a significant portion of your life, if not all your life, no matter how talented and driven you are, you may just end up never making your living at acting and always making it at something else. Your life has to be something you can live with independent of the acting—not something you're putting off "until you make it" because maybe you never will. And then maybe you will make it and realize you're now totally invested in a place you don't like any better now that you're being hounded by paparazzi than you did when you couldn't break your neck in front of an agent's office and get noticed. So make your life the way you want it, either here or in NY, and if you're happy that way, you'll be a success no matter what happens with your career.

As you can see, the LA vs. NY debate is a hot topic with many diverse opinions. In this thread, I found many great replies, one particularly from SE. Her response had a very strong impact on me. Through her thoughts I realized that success as an actor only matters if one is happy in their personal life. Sometimes we get so wrapped up in our ambitions that we forget to think about *all* the factors that make us happy.

As you may have guessed, my heart is in NY. Although the road may lead me to LA in the future, I know for now that NY is where I want to be. Three weeks is definitely not enough time to establish yourself as an actor in LA or anywhere for that matter, but it certainly is enough time to know whether or not you can live there. My thing is that I don't like to drive. I don't think I would have realized how much I don't like it if I hadn't made this trip. LA is a driving city. That is a fact. I can't be stressing out over the driving when I should be focusing on the audition or the shoot or the call back. It should just not be an issue. I know that in time I can adjust, but for me, at this stage of my career, I'd rather it not be a factor. A lot of you are probably thinking I'm crazy, but ultimately what makes the difference for me is that I am not just thinking about the driving factor, I am thinking about the *whole* picture. I am asking myself how important is it for me to be close to my family and friends, whether or not I can handle a long distance relationship with my boyfriend and on a lesser level, if I can handle dealing with traffic every day. For me, these are all factors that will truly make a difference in my decision. It all goes into the whole quality of life issue. As SE said, " . . . *establish yourself wherever you think you have the best chance of being personally happy.*"

Thursday, January 29, 2004

I had a really nice day today. It was one of those days when I could actually picture myself living here. Go figure—I start to feel it just when I'm about to leave! It's funny how that can sneak up on you. Just when I had my impressions of this city all mapped out in my head, I get a curve ball. I had lunch with my friend Donna and we talked about the biz all through lunch. It was a beautiful day and the sun was shining (actually, the sun has shined every day since I have been here) and I let myself take it all in. I was really starting to feel what it would be like to live here. Today was a good day. This day gave me a little glimpse of the lifestyle I'd have and it was nice. After all my anxieties about driving and living out here, it was very comforting to know that I can take that positive feeling back with me.

However, my decision is still to build more credits in NY and reevaluate my situation in six months, one year, etc. Although my choice right now is to go back to NY, LA will always be in the wings. My day with Donna was actually quite inspiring. Before we headed out to lunch, Donna showed me her reel and her screen tests for a popular soap opera. It was quite exciting to hear about the whole process—from first read to reading for the producers to callbacks and finally to the screen test. Donna currently has a recurring role on the soap and was able to share a lot of her insights on how she got the part. It made me realize how much work and phases go into preparing for the screen test and also how fast it can all happen. One great screen test and you can suddenly have a four year contract! That is quite an overwhelming and exciting thought. It happens all the time where you struggle for so many years, and then BAM, you nail the audition and callbacks, then you're screen testing, then you're signing a contract that'll set you up for several years! The funny thing is, she said a lot of the actors that reach the screen test are sometimes not very good. This is where the business gets so unpredictable. Donna was asked to screen test and read several boys up for a contract role. She said there were a few that totally missed the mark and she wondered how they ever made it to that phase. As most of us actors are aware, it can be the result of who you know or being at the right place at the right time, or more times than not, simply having the right look. The point is, getting to the screen test can happen to anyone. The goal is to be ready when it happens to you.

So with that in mind, the most important aspect of our conversation was the need to continue to take classes. Aside from Brette's Audition class, I hadn't been in a true scene study/ acting class in quite sometime. I know that a huge part of being a successful actor is to constantly be working—whether it is front of a camera or in front of a class so that when opportunities arise where you are asked to screen test, you know you can nail it. Donna asked if my trip to LA was worth it. YES, it was. There are many opinions about whether or not actors should go to LA and the bottom line is, each person has to find out for themselves. As I said earlier, many times you hear—don't go if you don't have an agent or don't go unless you have a job. Well, the heart of the matter is, every person's experience is going to be *different*. The best thing to do is to make the decision based on your own situation and then judge whether or not LA, NY, or Timbuktu is the right place for you. We make so many choices when it comes to acting, don't let this choice be someone else's.

I am so glad that I came and experienced LA for myself. If you're only going for a few weeks, don't make the trip about "getting discovered." Actors spend years here building relationships and still continue to struggle and work hard. For those of you planning a short-term stay, make the trip about discovering LA. See if you like the driving, the people, the nightlife, the neighborhoods, the weather, etc. As we addressed, one can only achieve true professional success when one is happy with their personal life taking into consideration all of the factors that comprise both. The two worlds must meet and be at peace with each other so that each can thrive individually. How can you go to an audition with a positive attitude if you are not happy being apart from a loved-one or if you are not happy with the where you live? This trip was a wonderful learning experience. It taught me how to plan, how to adjust in a new city, how to learn from mistakes, how to face challenges, but most importantly, it taught me how to be honest with myself—how to make decisions on what is best for me and my happiness.

Friday, January 30, 2004

Unbelievable!!!! Today is my last full day here in LA and wouldn't you know it—I got called for work from Central Casting for next week on the FOX show *Cracking Up* with Molly Shannon!!! When I first arrived here, I kept getting calls for work in NY and now that I head back, I'm starting to get calls for work in LA! So I'm sitting here slightly amused, but mostly in absolute amazement at the hilarity of it all. Plus, I'm really bummed!! It would have been great to be on an LA set. Why couldn't I have gotten this call last week! Well, I can go crazy with these thoughts or just let it go. This is only extra work—believe me I am not knocking extra work at all—it is often my bread and butter, however, in this case it would be at more cost for me to make arrangements to stay. If it were a call to audition for a pilot, that's a whole other ball game. I would absolutely make plans to stay longer. So this then teaches me another lesson—timing is everything. I should have expected this. I only made the commitment to stay for three weeks so this was bound to happen. I'm glad that I registered with these extras agencies with the hope that I could book work for the time that I was here, but realistically it's hard to predict when these companies will call. So my advice is, if you do register with these agencies, plan on being here at least three months or longer so that when they do call, you have a better chance of being available to accept the job. That advice also goes for building relationships. Although it may not be impossible, it is certainly difficult to settle in and expect to make contacts and work within a month. As I said earlier, *I was hopeful, but realistic* about my stay. If your main goal is to build relationships out here, then you really need to invest the time and that means sticking it out.

Saturday, January 31, 2004

So here I am, more than halfway through my flight back to New York and I feel a bit of sadness. What a journey this has been and what discoveries I have made about LA and about myself since I first wrote in this diary.

I know I have been anxious to get back home, but now as I sit here on a plane back to NY, a part of me wonders what the picture would have looked like if I had stayed a bit longer. This trip allowed me to get a little glimpse of that picture and for that the trip was well worth it. I am more motivated than ever to pursue this dream. Yes, LA is the pulse of the film and television industry. There is no doubt that the film and television opportunities in LA outnumber those in NY. If that's the answer you are looking for then yes, I think LA is the place to be. But my choosing NY was based on so many more factors. Yes of course, having opportunities would make me ecstatic, but the more honest I was with myself, the easier the decision became. Yes, I still strive to be a talented actress, but not at the expense of my personal happiness.

No matter what kinds of setbacks I experience while pursuing this dream, I know that it will not consume me because I have a life *outside* of the business that is fulfilling, with the peace of being where I want to be and sharing my highs and lows with the people I want to be near. I know that LA has a lot more to offer in terms of acting work, but NY for me has my family, my honey, my heart. Those were all factors that helped me make *my* decision. Other people will choose differently, but the point is to always be honest with yourself and know what's important to you. Know what will make the difference in your happiness.

As I say that, the flight attendant offers me a complimentary glass of Chablis (nice!) and as I take a sip of this lovely surprise treat, I am more than ever so glad to be heading home.

During this flight, our movie was *Under the Tuscan Sun* starring Diane Lane. As I watch this movie, the characters talk about crossroads and new beginnings. I found that to be quite appropo at this time as I just passed a crossroad and chose a path that was right for me. It is similar to the in-flight movie, *A View from the Top* when I headed out to LA where the message was "Don't let anything get in the way of your destiny." In that movie she too realized that there was more to being happy than fulfilling her dreams. Being happy was about seeing and living the *whole* picture. I know it sounds funny, but it's interesting how each movie to and from LA happened to effect me. I almost feel like I am being guided somehow.

I think about this trip and what it has meant to me. Throughout this journey I never knew what to expect or where the road led. In fact you could say the very same thing about acting. Lord knows it is a very unpredictable business. There was something Diane Lane's character said in this movie that truly made an impact on me, *"They say they built the train tracks over the Alps between Vienna and Venice before there was a train that could make the trip. They built it anyway."* How inspiring is that. It's all about taking a leap of faith.

We too are constantly building those tracks . . . taking classes, going on auditions, studying our craft . . . doing all of this without any certainty of success, but we do it because we have faith. We do it because we love it. No matter where you choose to fulfill your dream or what path you choose at your crossroad, always remember that *you will thrive where you are happy.* It takes a lot of guts to explore a new city from scratch. No can take that away from me. Having made this trip, I was able to answer a lot of questions about the lifestyle, the culture, neighborhoods, the driving, the people and so much more. I realized that I need and want to be close to my family and friends, that I didn't want a long distance relationship with my boyfriend, and I like taking the trains and walking all over the city as opposed to driving everywhere. These were just some of the things that I learned about myself that helped me decide that NY is where I want to be. I really wouldn't have discovered all that if I hadn't made the trip. At peace with this information, I found the answer I was looking for.

FINAL THOUGHTS

As actors we are constantly making choices that we hope are right for the characters we play. These choices cannot be made without doing the homework—asking the who, what, when, where and why's. We certainly shouldn't expect to do any less when it comes to choices that affect our own lives. To move or not to move to LA? Knowledge is power. I say if you are serious about moving, be sure to do your homework first. And always remember, you can be a success *anywhere* as long as you are happy and doing what you love.

www.ingramcontent.com/pod-product-compliance
Lightning Source LLC
Chambersburg PA
CBHW032136090426
42743CB00007B/616